The Hypocrisies
of
Heaven

Poems New & Old

by

Leo Yankevich

Books by Leo Yankevich

Collections

The Unfinished Crusade
The Last Silesian
Tikkun Olam (second edition)
Journey Late at Night

Chapbooks

The Language of Birds
Grief's Herbs (after Stanisław Grochowiak)
The Gnosis of Gnomes
Epistle from the Dark
The Golem of Gleiwitz

E-Books

Metaphysics
"You Who Live and Hear"
Tikkun Olam (first edition)

The Hypocrisies of Heaven

Poems New & Old

by

Leo Yankevich

Foreword by Sally Cook

Counter-Currents Publishing Ltd.
San Francisco
2016

Cover image:
Hieronymus Bosch, *The Conjurer*, circa 1502

Cover design by Leo Yankevich
Published in the United States by
COUNTER-CURRENTS PUBLISHING LTD.
P.O. Box 22638
San Francisco, CA 94122
USA
http://www.counter-currents.com/

Hardcover ISBN: 978-1-940933-76-4
Paperback ISBN: 978-1-940933-77-1
E-book ISBN: 978-1-940933-78-8

Library of Congress Cataloging-in-Publication Data

Names: Yankevich, Leo, author.
Title: The hypocrisies of heaven : poems new & old / by
Leo Yankevich ; foreword by Sally Cook.
Description: San Francisco : Counter-Currents Publish-
ing Ltd., 2016.
Identifiers: LCCN 2016030825 (print) | LCCN 2016036319
(ebook) | ISBN 9781940933764 (hardcover : alk. paper) |
ISBN 9781940933771 (pbk. : alk. paper) | ISBN
9781940933788 (ebook) | ISBN 9781940933498 (ebook)
Classification: LCC PS3625.A6795 A6 2016 (print) | LCC
PS3625.A6795 (ebook) | DDC 811/.6--dc23
LC record available at https://lccn.loc.gov/2016030825

Acknowledgments

Some of the poems in this collection first appeared in the
following journals:

Amelia, American Jones Building & Maintenance, Alternative Right, Artword Quarterly, Beauty for Ashes Poetry Review, Blue Unicorn, Candelabrum, Cedar Hill Review, Chronicles: A Magazine of American Culture, Counter-Currents/North American New Right, Contemporary Sonnet, Counter Punch, Disquieting Muses, Edge City Review, Electric Acorn, Envoi, FutureCycle Poetry, Harpstrings, Iambs & Trochees, Iota, Ironwood, Kimera, Lite: Baltimore's Literary Newspaper, Lucid Rhythms, Mr. Cogito, New Hope International, Nostoc, Parnassus Literary Journal, Pennine Platform, The Pittsburgh Post-Gazette, Poetry Nottingham, Poetry Salzburg, Psychopoetica, Raintown Review, Riverrun, Romantics Quarterly, Ship of Fools, Snakeskin, Shatter Colors Literary Review, Sonnet Scroll, Staple, Sulphur River Literary Review, Tennessee Quarterly, The Barefoot Muse, The Chimaera, The East River Review, The Eclectic Muse, The Flea, The Innisfree Poetry Journal, Loch Raven Review, The London Magazine, The MacGuffin, The Monongahela Review, The Neovictorian/Cochlea, HyperTexts, The Shit Creek Review, The Pennsylvania Review, The Sarmatian Review, The Tennessee Review, Tucumcari Literary Review, Trinacria, Visions International, Washington Literary Review, Weyfarers, Whelks Walk Review, Windsor Review,
inter alia.

Contents

Foreword by Sally Cook

Leo Yankevich rages at the grid in which we find ourselves entrapped. Recognizing commonalities based on natural experience, his deep disgust with deception forces him to look directly at a world in which leaves are charred, skies leaden, death frequent, love absent, and good ambiguous. *The Hypocrisies of Heaven* is his journal in verse, an open book unto himself.

Yankevich is an illuminator, a poet with deeply held convictions. As a creative artist, he can do nothing else but build a framework for his perceptions and be faithful to them. Let us set aside the old argument of *politics vs. poetry*, and marvel at the insight displayed in the poems "Flags" and "Do Not Shed Tears for the Drowned Boys." He honestly poses questions about politics, genealogy, citizenship, religion, and any topics we are told not to discuss by our handlers. He views them all from a larger world perspective than that of a politically correct mosquito, and achieves a narrative which is neither manufactured, nor life-diminishing. He takes a truly universal and encompassing stance from which he is able to assess and comment on anything he observes: family, nature, racial characteristics, sex; even his bad liver and possible weight gain are put under scrutiny. He is merciless, even when it comes to himself. Though my conclusions don't always interlock with his, as a poet I have continued to learn from this master technician and rock-solid individual.

An oracle for our time, he often comes to dark and devastating conclusions. That is his way. He knows what true poets through the ages have always known, and joins them in viewing the grittiness of life. And then he will suddenly turn to flying his kite or joining with eagles to record in unique, always fresh detail, flashes of deep empathy and great beauty of which lesser bards can only dream. He is the poet so many have wished to be.

While a few poems are couched in obscurity, no amount of head-in-the-sand posturing can blur his truths. Those who look beneath the surface will marvel at runes "wrought from strife." I find this book to be an endless well of thought, joy, and reflection. Read it.

—Sally Cook, May 18, 2016

After Hieronymus Bosch

The day exits through dusk, the sun on hills
angry at its going. Briar and brush,
in death, like spring against the twill of fields,
through limbs and leaves amid hunger and hush,
obey the wind on whims of winter's will.
Old men sigh in the shade; God wags his beard;
and like a Judas goat before the kill,
time buries its head in the wake of fear.
The moon hangs in the lull; the blazing spears
blunt the eclipse above the pyramid;
mummies rise in the mind; fey frozen tears
blaze like beacons above the boiling lid;
in the light: soul hugs the eternal now,
redeemed, not knowing when or why or how.

2000

A Hundred since the First
(August 2014)

For five days the blowflies have cleansed their bones.
Now they lie waiting for the August rain,
for holy water, afterlives beyond Ukraine,
sure heaven neither judges nor atones?

Atop *tarn* uniforms, their sun-bleached skulls
resemble cauliflowers amid rapeseed,
fodder for architects and lords of greed
who build Earth's fences and tear down Earth's walls.

No second coming for these meek and poor,
no Christ to lean on, anti-christ to blame—
they mistake fuse for wick and pray to flame
we're not on the eve of the third world war.

All We've Been Told

I can recall her bent back in the garden,
staking tomato plants and raking soil;
in winter, when the bitter earth would harden,
shovelling the ice and snow, her toil

remembered only by blue jays; and, come
the summer, sitting in her yard with clothes
clean on the drooping lines; how she would hum
and sing in Calabrese and cut a rose.

Those candy handouts during Halloween,
the corn wreath hung upon her spotless door
were both a cryptic question and an answer.

Was she once lovely on the silent screen,
and the best dancer on the parquet floor?
All we've been told is that she died of cancer.

A Magic Mountain

It comes to this: a greyness like no other
under clouds uncanny as the mist.
And down below, the village church so small
its Sunday bells on Monday reach the crest.

And leafless trees descending to the river,
melting snowmen lined against the wall
where shelters stronger than your lack of faith
await the never-ending miracle.

And suddenly it burns a living gold
beyond the scope of any oracle.
And you forget your pain, forget your death,
and greet the ghost that has you in its hold.

Angels & Demons

1

When an angel stretches his hands
across the entire universe,
he touches us as we our pets.
He has already won the game,
innumerable light years ahead.

2

And if there are angels, demons exist,
stretching their venom and their talons
through black holes, devouring time,
space, matter, torturing dogs and cats,
not touching us, but eating hearts.

Archie Bunker Rhymes

A cuckservative* wooed the vote of Diego,
and married a dwarf from south of Laredo.
The Koch brothers offered him a lump,
and then along came Donald Trump
to put an end to pinko correctness.
Careless with words? The effect was:
the return of our beloved free speech,
and fewer burritos on the beach.

*Jeb Bush

Ark

They built each city and each dam,
perfected their technology
to master heaven, earth and sea,
in love with money, Marx, or Lamb?

Yet, all we've dug up and see now
are ruins, wrecks and skeletons,
black plastic garbage bags by tons,
a billboard with a smiling cow.

Their love, hate, honour and disgrace?
—abstractions to us who've come far
across time, galaxy and star.
We're not piqued by the human race.

Their lives and actions mean as much
as those of cockroaches, snails and ants.
How ugly they are without pants.
We've come here not to preach or touch.

The humble, pious and the meek
still clinging in their graves to faiths
are real to us as ghosts or wraiths
that lived a century or a week.

Yes, we have closed the book on that,
the denizen of house and mall,
and saved the worthiest of all,
each species and each breed of cat.

A Tree & Its Fruit
(September 2015)

Those who have come ashore
are neither meek nor poor.

Invaders to your land,
they mock the helping hand.

They "go" to Germany,
where homes and food are free,

where Merkel gives dictates
to all the weaker states.

Part guinea pig, part cow,
she could teach Hitler how.

Awe

A leaf, perhaps the last,
breaks from a maple tree,
spins in the chilly blast
of November, floating free

before it hits a wall,
attempts to run and leap,
only to quickly fall
onto a mounting heap

of others, stop, and fade.
No one admired its fight
with wind, and no one made
a chronicle of its flight.

It lies anonymous.
No one recalls or grieves.
It's one of numerous
other autumn leaves.

No one saw what you saw
that moment in the sun.
No one stood there in awe.
You were the only one.

Before His Majesty

A little vague, so very touched, he sits
with mouth agape, and he regards the men
in white as they unknot his mind with straps,
as they unsicken—free his soul with pins.

The pins feel bad, unlike the flames that fly
in pastures, suns atop a crimson barn,
the straw inside a bed for dreams, the dumb
at prayer, at prayer. Amid the solemn dust,

the horses neighing, childhoods gone amuck,
the wheel of torture turns like heresy.
The Law redeems no-one. The courts exist
for glory, glory. . . mid so much mercy.

Buk near Donetsk
(August 2014)

Beside the fields of rye and flax
there is a road that leads to birches,
pocked with dark puddles and tank tracks,
above which no white dove perches.

Green men pray to another Christ,
a Fulcrum falling overhead,
a saviour or a poltergeist,
the sun behind it, fierce and red.

Caterpillar

For fifteen days a caterpillar feeds
on sorrel, selfheal, ragwort, mint, or privet.
If a wasp mounts it and injects its larvae,
they'll prosper on its blood, and then gnaw through

its epidermis, fragile in the weeds.
The woolly bear will suffer trauma, outlive it,
protect the wasp cocoons, and then starve three
weeks, though surrounded by lush leaves and dew.

This is not part of a conspiracy.
The female wasp does what she's always done.
The hapless caterpillar does the same.

And so it is with people; few are free
to fly away as Coppers in the sun,
Monarchs or moths in unforgiving flame.

Cats

No creatures are as fine as cats,
asleep perfectly on armchairs,
in the wake of more curtain tears.
The gifts they bring: toads, sparrows, rats!

And how they know the shingled roof,
the long arms of an ancient elm,
with lives that never overwhelm.
Perhaps that's why they're so aloof.

Immortalized by Rilke, Blake,
companion to old cranks and spinsters,
to janitors and prime ministers,
they're there to greet you when you wake.

Céline

Three pamphlets in which he spared none
do not diminish my esteem.
Rats in a stable are not horses.
(How well he knew their beady eyes,
steaming sewers and twisted knives!)

The pamphlets are medals on his chest,
pearls of truth upon his canon,
while the gnawed brown beams of Europe
crumble in the metro slums
and France relents once more, and burns.

Cemetery

I hold a fist full of earth in my hand,
breathe in its sweet smell. Sweat drips down my brow,
as I carefully fill a rusty can
for flowers, using a sucked thumb as plow.

Years go by like this: I repeat the work
of my mother, make heaven out of clay.
In the immense shadow of a black stork,
I kneel, mumble words she taught me to say.

1993

Chelsea Hotel 1986

You rise and wipe a dream from sleepless eyes.
You pour a drink and look out at the world.
Again the leaves must die flamboyantly,
the minstrels from the Andes play their flutes.

Your liver hurts. You pour another drink.
The bottle soon is empty. Sadness real.
You're twenty-five years old and still alive.
You make a note to scorn all medicos.

You have been dying at a subtle pace.
You look outside, up at the orange light
that gives a meaning to the passing clouds.
You have grown hard, then soft, then hard again.

You touch her breasts and pour another drink.
Her hips are wide and round as Saturn's moons.
You kiss her on her back, then on her neck,
and you have her as if she were your life.

Childhood Leaves

Their smoke obstructed the October sun
and burnt our throats and brought tears to our eyes.
One time we went behind the backyard shed
to see who freed them, kites into our skies.
Some still aflame, some charred, some brownish dun,
they rose into a heaven made of lead.

Chronos

Do you remember when we stopped:
the corner of Fifth and Twenty-Third,
to kiss and dry-fuck, leaves of Indian
Summer mocking each passionate word?

And how we wore the rags of that age,
our parents heavy in each thumb,
advising us in the wake of failures,
as if our love was malt and rum?

And how we bade goodbye in August,
lifetimes before us, young forever,
and now you, post-menopausal,
I, wobbling towards the rusty lever?

Cirrhosis

Edema set in now,
ankles and belly swollen—
the future past looks foul,
the self soon to be fallen.

Yet, the will lifts the feet,
and carries umpteen years
down the stairs to the street
for only ten more beers.

Then, the return, ascent—
four stories up the stairs
to white walls and the rent,
the heights and the lament.

Come a Day of Deeds & Doom

Come a day of deeds and doom upon a scale,
and every duped codger will dawn a smile
on a horizon wet with rainbows, and hail
how, to his relish, every gesture's a guile

as whimmed as the wind that had borne him sorrow;
then will cast his thoughts to an unminding ear
and haply down a drink of wry tomorrow
as again a new creed and ethic draw near;

and tossing his scroll of skin and new-made mask
into the same self-devouring sea,
with each salty human tear again will ask,

look, and find: a picture-perfect paradise—
that never was or is—but just might be
along the cracked mirror of his burning eyes.

1996

Computer Programmer
(Age 36, Single Looking For Woman)

This is the end, a dead end, some might say,
the end of the road never taken. Frost's
or yours, or mine. This road leads round a grey
bend like imagined fumes from mute exhausts,
like fumes that never rise or kill the air.
We take it, and we find there are no costs,
other than what we hope for, or despair.

He sits outside his house, inside his car,
looking like a peeping-Tom at what
will never happen: nights of warmth and charms,
a honeymoon spent tropical and far.
Yet in his dither it's himself he harms.
No, he will never turn the key or cut
the corner to a night within her arms.

Counter-Attack

On 27 January 1945 the Red Army had just been defeated in an armour engagement with the 20th Panzer Division, which was retreating to escape encirclement slightly south of Gleiwitz in Upper Silesia. Two villages were punished for the defeat: Preiswitz, populated by Poles, and neighbouring Schönwald, populated by Germans. In total, 200 innocent civilians were murdered in cold blood.

The sniped T-34s blaze in the snow,
some with their upturned turrets venting smoke,
others with gaping holes from each fierce blow.
The Red infantrymen begin to choke—
a Mongol, Tatar, Uzbek, Ket, and Jew,
the last who holds a pistol to the ear
of a young Pole whose eyes are black and blue,
who'll not forget the day, or month or year.

Now Schönwald's Germans must endure their wrath.
Whole families are lined against brick walls,
girls raped and fathers beaten on the path
that leads to where another village falls.
And no amount of soap in history's bath
can make them clean, or let us hear their calls.

Dante's Inferno

Looking down into the eaves,
looking for God
in the glare of icicles,
I found the resting place of evil,
found hell and the devil:
a silver dime and two nickels,
a stream of clotted mud,
and a host of forgotten leaves.

1996

Deep Sleep

Deep, deep sleep at 54
is better than sex at 20.
No expectations,
only the eagerness
to meet parents and siblings.
No orgies, only love fests.

Distant Kin

They lived in far-off lands and cities—
spread across a spinning globe—
never-met uncles, aunts and cousins,
long-since buried in my mind.

My father mourned them in his cups
as "cancer," "heart-attack," and "stroke"
stuck in his larynx like blunt arrows
to dim the living room at noon.

The boy in me still sees the arrows
mirrored in the whisky lakes.
And in my eyes their distant lives
are limned by agony and grief.

Do not Shed Tears
for the Drowned Boys

Do not shed tears for the drowned boys
like flotsam on the Turkish shores.
Free from their fathers' stupidity,
their wings bear the Trojan horse
to the ruins of antiquity
and to the altruistic Norse.

Weep rather for the fair-haired boys
and for the blue and green-eyed girls,
your grandsons and your great granddaughters
with tiny fingers in yellow curls?
There will be no baptismal waters,
only fire drowning out their worlds.

Dream: Milosz

Milosz lies on his death bed,
but, on the other side,
awake in a grey room

where there's no night or day—
a Swedenborgian
self-sentenced heaven-hell.

I stand nearby the window.
He says: "I've always known
I am the greatest poet."

I answer: "I feel the same
about my humble self.
And what about God?"

With stern hawkish eyes,
he looks at me and says:
"Electricity! "

Dying Breed

He plays by rules
no longer on the books,
        brags his verse tools
descend from Cleanth Brooks.

He names each friend:
Dick Wilbur, Tony Hecht,
        asks them to send
a blurb, like an insect.

Thin-lipped Tim Murphy,
his time on earth is done.
        He is not worthy
of a place in the sun.

Poor Jared Carter
who never learned to rhyme,
        try, try, try harder:
you'll both be cleansed by time.

Earth

There is no mercy here.
The sun beats down on pity,
tears reenter clouds,
and rainfall floods a city.

Elegy for Hanns Breitenbach
(1890-1945)

You disappeared in the dead of winter,
but not like Yeats. No wife or mistress
was at your side. A hole and splinter
alarmed you, but did not distress.

Duty called. You would not part
your sculptor's studio, the stench
of war not keep you from your art,
from rasps and chisels on your bench.

Dressed in a motorcycle coat
to warm you in the bitter cold,
you did not cower in fear or gloat.
You stood by your files and mould.

The Bolshies gave you a lead fan,
a spray of Marx across the chest.
They took you for an SS man,
and heaped your body with the rest.

Elysium

It is a wrinkle
or a rill
I've journeyed down.

The only light
was Artemis,
there for the kill—

my good and bad
led into night
past slaughterhouse
and leafy hill

to where a boy
waits with his kite,
no more at odds
with his own will.

Esse

"And if he should have to compete with those who
had been always prisoners, by laying down the law
about those shadows while he was blinking before
his eyes were settled down—and it would take a
good long time to get used to things—wouldn't
they all laugh at him and say he had spoiled his
eyesight by going up there, and it was not worth-
while so much as to try to go up? And would they
not kill anyone who would try to release them and
take them up, if they could somehow lay hands on
him and kill him?"
"That they would!" said he. (Socrates)
—from Book VII of Plato's *The Republic*

To be a little touched, the sacred way:
in slants of light that glorify windows.
To be a tad estranged, unlike all those
who smile as guiltless gods against the grey

twilight, bursting to flame, bursting to flame.
To be, to be, beyond the cage of be-
ing, court, arbiter, jury, holy see—
nor here nor there, imbecilically lame

in that august mystery and graven mood.
To be, a moment, still as stone, bright stone
that's grasped like truth, alone amid the lone,
though hoisted high upon a crimsoned rood.

Every Turncoat

Every turncoat has his reason,
fear of the left, rejections from
publishers that promote his treason,
loss of fortune. Under thumb
he is, limited in what he writes,
all-inclusive in his view.
He sees crime, not Blacks killing Whites,
and never does he name the Jew.

Erotic Dreams

In every erotic dream I'm twenty-six;
the beauty next to me the same or younger.
Eight inches stand proud with no need for licks.
At fifty-four there isn't any hunger;
and yet the old man stands as if by rote.
Absurd, insane, he will not wear a coat.

8 June 2016

Farewell

Do not look back.
The swamp's aflame.
Forget each crack
in the rigged game.

Forget the cousin
flawed to the bone.
One in a dozen
can't fend alone.

Unable, old,
they'd made their mess.
Facing the cold,
they now confess.

It's bitter Earth
we leave below.
A mudshark's worth,
can but get low.

The commie has
his paradise:
hip-hop and jazz,
Kool-Aid and ice.

Farm Animals

Pity them, eyes innocent
inside the coop, the old red barn,
the stable... but do not lament.
Their lives are less than hay and scarn.

We carry them inside our bowels,
blood, flesh, sinew, prostate and brain.
Their whimpers are our cries and howls,
fur and feathers in the rain.

Signs and symbols of our sorrow,
the knife and hatchet cancel birth.
No, they have no far-off tomorrow.
They'll die here on the dying earth

along with our old architecture,
dialects, fads, fashions, art.
They will not know the odd, strange texture,
of our hosts after we depart.

Festung Breslau, 1945

Eight-hundred years have passed
  since Mongols scaled the walls,
their faces scalded, a fireball cast
  upon their backs, their calls

unheeded by mute *Tengri*,
  their father in the sky.
Yet they fled with the head of Henry,
  maids in each slanted eye.

Now with tanks they return,
  surrounding *Festung Breslau*.
Townhouses collapse, and streetcars burn.
  The Khazar lays down his law.

Pity the carrion,
  the corpses on balconies,
the ruins unwoken by the sun,
  the mother on her knees.

Fin de Siècle

1

The rail I once clung to, clung to like hope,
is flaking away in the autumn rain.
And now my feet ache when they touch the stair.
God of the far clouds, have you no mercy?

The rooks, the fat hungry rooks—caw, caw, caw
in the yellow smoke of smouldering leaves,
and not even the rats, brave bastards now,
not even the rats, scurry for shelter.

2

This is my kingdom of thistles and thorns,
my mustard seed that never took root,
and so what, so what, says Milton's devil,
so what, so what, the disillusioned heart.

We are at the brink of a brave new world,
at the brink of wonderful new freedoms!
Let us stuff all our insatiable bowels
with joysticks and mice, and stab a foetus!

3

"Eli, Eli, lama sabach'thani?"
I say unto a snickering shadow.
If there were but angels to wrestle with,
let them humble my body into flame

that a soul might rise up out of the ash!
"Hoo-hoo!" say all the monkeys in God's head.
"Through all the salt seas on your burning tongue
we've already lived all the lives you've led."

1999

Flags
(June 2015)

Gay Pride is raised, and Dixie's down.
The Kenyan king inside his House
has it lit to reflect his crown.
Ms Jenner's teats swell in her blouse.

Burrs prick the sky in Baltimore;
more melons ripen in the South.
The US of old is no more.
The racist straight must shut his mouth.

We are all now Confederate,
with midnight spangled overhead,
although beyond, cold, temperate,
the stars say the dawn will be red.

For My Brother

I went out amid the melancholy
of paper cups and dead leaves,

went out for I no longer remember what.
The smell of stale beer and fried liver

lingered in my mind, and I thought of you, Alex,
but my empathy for you was too worn out,

so I abandoned you there in the closed ward.
We all live with loss, I thought, and walked on

to where I am now, on a bridge called time,
rusty like the old cars heaped in your yard,

like the door you never painted. The stream
is like a crow-black mirror, and the sun,

it just keeps on shining no matter what.
If I jump, will the mirror break my fall?

1994

From Amoeba to Man

"Every living being is an engine geared to the wheel-
work of the universe. Though seemingly affected only
by its immediate surroundings, the sphere of external
influence extends to infinite distance."—Nikola Tesla

So it is. From amoeba to man,
out of the mire, up to the skies.
And so it is on a strange planet
orbiting a distant star.

The paradigmatic two eyes
crawl out of the indifferent water,
the wide lungs of a dinosaur,
the father, mother, son and daughter

of the first mammal in his jaws.
A billion years will likely pass
before they walk on their two feet,

a billion more if they amass
sharp tools and swords and written laws,
a billion more until we meet.

Girl & Maid

The window mirrors transcendental light,
the sun at twelve o'clock, unseen but there,
the buds of two small breasts exposed to brightness
in a room imbued with balms and prayer.

The sconce as old as lofty trees outside
that stand like sentries as the wind forays,
accuses mute eternity in stride
below a veil of wax reflecting rays.

The girl beneath the quilt is dying, braid
removed from view. And yet the ticking clock
has long since stopped its ticking, and her maid

has long since joined her. Under tarnished lock
and key they lie, absorbed in solemn thought,
in photos I've not taken, but let fade.

Gleiwitzer Engel

Cinders in my eyes block out the view.
Still, past the dirty sills and sooty façade,
I look up and discover his noble face:
the corner of the fifth floor, on a street
the exiled forgotten Germans called *Löschstraße.*

Grey Wolves

At midnight they descend the hill,
(fur and flesh caught between their teeth),
howling at the moon and stars,
delighting in the knee-deep snow,
and in the purity of the pack,
while the wise red fox hunts alone.

Heaven

Piss in the bucket:
foam on the top,
sand on the bottom.
Docs say I've got
a kidney stone,
while I implore
I've got a diamond.

Hedgehog

Beneath the rowan berry,
the mackerel midnight,
with dew upon its snout,
foe to the frog and beetle,

always in the corner
of grey tabby cat eyes,
it greets me as if Plato
in the cave, I with beer

deposit bottles, and belly
graveyards towards heaven
that only I can people
in Hades or at home.

Here Comes a Commie

He's Che Guevara
underneath his red beret.
　　　He's Leon Trotsky
with his belly full of bagels,

　　　this man, this very
sensitive man, so finely bred
　　　on Marx and Marcuse
who sits over cups of steaming

　　　cappuccino,
butt-hole tight from doing kegels,
　　　mouth sore from nights
spent moaning, from days spent dreaming

　　　of equality
for every woman, black, and gay,
　　　and all the ghetto
commissars inside his head.

Hilda

1

Few see what she sees
in the corner of her eyes:
a flood of refugees
who gawk and proselytize.

No multiculturalist,
a dagger in her purse,
the only man she's kissed
is blond and blue-eyed Ernst.

2

How long will the smell of rain
and refugees linger in the train?

They've gotten off, and yet the stink
of the Levant wed to the ink

of bureaucrats hangs like a map
on station walls. The pup on her lap

gags and growls at the ghosts of some,
for it knows, knows what is to come.

Hillary & Bill

"Pegging is when you wear a strap-on dildo and pene-
trate your guy." — Jill Hamilton, *Cosmopolitan Maga-
zine*, Jan 19, 2016

Poor Hillary was about to kill
right after the Lewinsky affair.
Her cheating husband, blowjob Bill,
was standing in his underwear,

explaining what took place, and begging
for sex, which he hadn't had in weeks.
"All right, I'll give you a good pegging.
Bend over and open those two cheeks!"

Dressed only in a big strap-on
resembling Bill's unsmoked cigar,
she pounded him from dusk to dawn
as agents sat in the Clinton car,

on the look-out for paparazzi.
Thus, long before it was in fashion,
before her e-mails and Benghazi,
she'd buggered him, rekindling passion.

Hospice

Dawn of pewter, nary a cloud.
A city dove alights the cypress,
the forsythia touches the moon.

Of all the signs of the zodiac
cancer rises over her brow,
wrinkled for thirty-seven years.

Then the constellation fades,
the sun burns the weeds on the lawn
until suddenly they are green.

How to Get to Heaven

Pauline sang like an angel in the choir,
her blue eyes looking heavenward, far past
the stained-glass windows. Yet I laid her fast.
My balls and manhood were her body's sire.

Her lips were soft, tumescent, from being pleasured,
her subtle thanks for thrusts both deep and strong.
Her delicate hands said she liked it long.
My smacks on her pale ass cheeks were well measured.

She lay with nature's love inside her womb,
both yoni and nipples swollen, soul content.
I laid her, too, before and after Lent.

Saints on the window never leave the tomb.
My grandson's knocking at his angel's door,
for God loves when her panties hit the floor.

Icarus

I have beheld the moon eclipse the sun
but I am no blinder in my blindness.

My headlong plunge in the pain-lacquered well,
my ecstatic leap through the flames of silence,

couldn't kill the self-devouring mare,
this sickness giving suck to desire.

Yet I prayed hope was more than wax and wings
and soared beyond faith, even though I fell.

1999

In Fear

Something's at it again
    in the hollow
of my heart,
    black
    as the crow
of sorrow.

And once again
    the stillness
of the Lord
        mid His holy
impending shadow,
        festers in the wound
    of a captured word.

Abba,
  humble my ache,
if you can,
    before my hunger
    steals another hymn
from Eden's tree,
    or Jesu's bleeding hand.

With half a wing,
  I am but breath and sin
    caged in this boon
the joyful savants
        call life.

  Trembling,
    I place it before you
like a rune—
    wrought from strife.

In the Still Sad Shade

In the still sad shade a nettle prospers,
far from the son's fury and lilting light.
Rails rust and words lie low, fallen from heights
of pride and bravado. Only whispers

whimmed by the wind fall from the lips of leaves,
dead or dying. All comfort's under clouds
grey and melancholy, under a shroud
of ash, where a withered crone weeps and grieves

for what was and for what might have been. I
would enter the light, but the heart says no,
in love with belladonna and shadow,

I would repent, disclaim the slag-hued sky,
but the self milks monotony, suckles
poisonous paps, childlike amid thistles.

1994

Karpatia

Piss in the old man's pail,
young raven on the sill,
half moon carved out of pewter,
the stars cruel as the night.

Karpatia forgives,
like Jesu on the wall,
but not the wolves, the vipers,
the flies, the maggots, time.

Kasia

In the dark at the corner
of her quavering eye:
this dawn walks upon
the blue waters of her iris.

1997

Kitten

The clouds are never quite the same.
This dusk they're mackerel with rooks
delighting far as the eye can see.
Yet here below, the same starved kitten,
(as I take out a bag of garbage),
behind a rusty iron gate,
waits for its tiny sachet of food.

Last Night the Moon

Last night the moon suddenly knocked me cold.
And I found myself amid cobblestones,
in a pool of urine, babbling prayers
till the ghost of the man I'd be—crawled out.

I lay like a drowned bull after a flood,
stiff, stiff, so stiff, yet freed from the struggle,
and watched the stars stone his gullible eyes
like tiny specks of Siberian salt.

And he wept to God and cursed the devil,
but I was numb, was too damn dead to help.
By dawn he was scavenging with the rats,
was digging amid my ribs for a soul.

1998

Lazarus

I came back, the wind whistling in my ear,
dove on my elbow, crow on my torn cuff,
but I could not remember; the long lost year
having left the hourglass like the love

that sifted through my hands less able now.
Dry mouth my only friend and fiercest foe,
I wobbled past each flowering branch and bough,
neuropathy on fire from sole to toe.

Lightning in a bottle lit my way
to where the moss was lush upon the stones,
and crosses mocked the many shades of grey,
the shadows over my skin, skull and bones.

Leo

You can forget him, the zoom
of his eyes, each metaphor,
the depth of his deep voice,
a lion now by choice,
for he's a man no more.
He wakes in a white room,
the sun white through the blind,
white and bright through the mind.

Letter to a Minister

Get out, get out,
you leftist rat!
and do not pout:
there where you sat—
the stink of a lout,
one who had shat
and cast no doubt,
his wallet fat.

There'll come a day
when you will go.
No scouts will lay
wreaths in the snow—
your traitorous head
beneath a steeple,
Marxist red
before the people.

Looking for . . .

A wench to spend time with on sultry nights,
one who knows when to open and to shut
her lovely mouth, and who demands no rights,
at church a saint, in bed a little slut.

A wench who bends, when like a maddened bull,
I mount her from behind. One who expects
and needs her sweet pudenda stretched and full,
lips later puffy, mind at ease from sex.

A wench who'll make and serve a hearty dinner
because she knows I am her special guest,
her alpha-male, her soul and body's winner,
a cocky cut above the meager rest.

A wench who never is too far or near
and knows precisely when to serve me beer.

Martial Law, Poland, 1982

It was a time of greyness and of tanks,
of water cannons on the market square,
a time of strikes, protests, and fear. Despair
was a catchword we wore to work, the thanks
we gave for empty shelves, for brothers crushed
beneath the muddy wheels of ZOMO lorries,
the finger we would give to those, who, storeys
above us, smiled, then kept our voices hushed.

It was a time of all resistance smashed,
of vodka in our wounds and cigarette
smoke in our eyes—of promises rehashed.
It was a time of snitches, thugs on call,
of bravery, of kindness, of regret—
a time of praying—and—no hope at all.

Mercy

The hour the mice climb out of the walls
is rancid joy, a bitter, bitter truth.
There is no crucifix wrapped round his thumb,
only paroxysms, otherworldly
thirst, and an inaudible psalm bleeding.
In the well of a flagon he beholds
white horses, the spleenish ghosts of the drowned
rising through the dregs. And only the sun
on the sallow roof reminds him of time
circling a contradictory globe.
Verily, he is at the blue threshold
where the lamp's affixed to eternity
and light pours down on an afflicted child
through the skeleton of a trembling leaf.

2000

Micky the Cat

Castrated at six months old,
he sits on the ninety year old
art deco green arm-chair,
a king upon a throne,
proud, beloved, alone—
futureless, sans heir.

I, his wise dying god,
watch from the corridor,
put down the small food plate,
thinking of the wad
that stabs me if paid late,
and keeps me sad and poor.

Mirror

The last time you looked in the mirror was
how many hours or years ago? You were
a handsome bastard then. No cough or buzz
in your ear bothered you. There wasn't a burr
beneath your skin. Your face beamed with raw youth
and you could make girls smile with just a grin.
Now wrinkles mark your brow and a dead tooth
stands out in the crowd. Your ear is tin,
though once you could sing like a man who knew
why he got up or even sang at all.
Your hair is silver, and up on the shelf
gold liquor is the sun, the love that you
could never betray. And suddenly it's fall.
Are you a fallen leaf? You forget yourself.

Mortimer

Always in the sea of his eyes
there is a glimmer of earnest pain.
No miracle's ever touched him,

no angel's whispered in his ears
inside a well-intentioned cliché,
no knock at 5 a.m.

has ever made him doubt his doubt,
the architecture of his logic,
the beauty of his ways.

Out on the porch tonight he stands
alone against the Pharisees,
the Romans, and the stars.

Mother Europe

Smoke in the alley of her love,
rank smouldering rags inside a barrel,
as swarthy Syrians push and shove,
like Moors of old, determined, feral.

They'll raise the crescent, kill the dove,
till "Allah Akbar" drowns our carol.
Our children will learn soon enough,
in Europe, foolish, vain and sterile.

Mountain Meditation

A hundred years from now I won't be here
amid these trees aglow with morning light.
It is enough for me that they'll be here,
their leaves a nameless colour at this height.

Mystic

He'd reached the crest and rested in the sun.
Glory, glory tolled the bells below.
A hawk descended over spruces—dun
eyes focused on a flutter in the snow.

And he beheld a dove ascending, blood
baptizing crowns beneath the vise of claws.
And in a wince he felt the final thud
of mercy—bless the stringency of laws.

Nature's Bible

God loves the meek as little as the thief.
He takes the victors, losers left with prayer.
But do not whimper, weep, lament or grieve;
his creatures must do or die everywhere.
Be it on a blue planet, a green leaf—
stars, stars away—a black hole is his stare.

Nazis

I had first learned about them from the black
& white flicks made back in the 1940s.
They wore strange monocles and spoke kraut English,
broken, guttural with hints of Yiddish.

I watched reruns, astonished at their lack
of kindness, how they killed their enemies.
They clicked their black boots, eager to extinguish
them like rats in a sewer, weak and skittish,

on their way to *Night of the Generals*,
where they grew faint when viewing decadent art,
where they would murder whores to get their kink,
malignant, always evil, on the throes

of madness; and then on to other roles,
in *Battle of the Bulge*, *The Train*, the part
of "I-know-nothing" Schultz, and Colonel Klink,
there on the backlot set of *Hogan's Heroes*.

Nettle Tea

On the black river's shore a nettle
prospers in the bracken shade.
The underside of the iron bridge
spans both the water and the glade.
Rusty as a pipe or kettle,
ghost trains traverse rails to a ridge

where folks set in their ways age cheese,
keg beer and eat perpetual stew.
The milk and malt stored in wood vats,
the deep bowls of brown broth and rue,
the honey and the combs of bees,
are guarded by a glare of cats,

and, in a cup, brews nettle tea,
hot, medicinal, with a cloud
of steam baptizing the high ceiling,
while nightfall, like a tattered shroud,
embraces dew on the green lea,
a windowpane of stars and healing.

No-Land's Season

Yester-morrow, a storm beyond the curtain
conveyed forgotten smells: flint and sulphur by rote,
while a hunchback, clad in grief, bore his burden
through a mirror, from salty pillar to post.

A dimension away, brine from my brow burned
his vision. And he shed the proverbial tears
of reptiles, knowing no-land's season would turn
like a wheel in a rut in a land without tears.

Spiders and snakes abounded, and were beloved
by the indifferent-to-the-world-of-men breeze.
And toads, crows and nettles were old friends, begrudged
by no thing, this side of hell's stretching boundaries.

These denizens had lived like druids during Lent—
carousing in dives, or toiling in solitude
over slabs of paper, canvas and stone. Spent
now, they aimlessly congregated, drank, and knew...

From timelessness to timelessness they'd sometimes jest,
look up at the forsaking sky, heed the silence,
repeat their falls, then each climb back into its nest,
comforted by the mercy of Karma's sentence.

1996

No Still Life

Marvel at the moon
resting on the gate,
feeding on ripe apples,
drinking midnight dew.

Giant eyes of owls
follow their small prey.
White hares in the brush
resurrect the leaves.

Old Anthology
(for a Forgotten Poet)

I found your name between Cawein and Clare
in the index of an old anthology,
which I had bought for only half a buck
while hunting classics at an open fair.
Your contribution is "The Morning Rook,"
a sonnet Williams chose to overlook
when filling up his *Little Treasury*.
It seems that even now you have no luck.
Today few know your only published book
or read your out-of-print biography.
And yet those fourteen chiseled lines were placed
beneath your name to last beyond your time,
as if their words could never be replaced
by prose, or gestures at a pantomime.

On Dying

Céline was right. Some people die
for twenty years, some in the splendour
of a second. So I lie
with body spent, my psyche tender

as Europe falls beneath the weight
of one more wave of dark invaders.
I've had my beer, and have my fate,
my liver fraught with scars and craters.

And yet the moralists in Brussels,
with their forked tongues and beady eyes,
their gall and bureaucratic muscles,
prod my way to paradise.

Our Poor Eyes

Only the Jew
is free to criticize
   himself and you.
Never does he tell lies.

He's sacrosanct,
a Hebrew *übermensch*
   who won't be spanked.
Forget his Auschwitz stench,

forget his cries:
only Polaks and Germans
   tell tall-lies.

Old Jew-boy sermons
that a Reb determines
   are our poor eyes.

Paean

A blue elf's smile on the surface of milk
in a bowl is pleasant delirium,
much nicer to look at than blood on silk,
than a spider bellowing kingdom come.

If I could understand the words of wood,
crucified with nails, I'd say that it hurts
to be wood, but wouldn't be understood
except, perhaps, by lizards wearing skirts.

The world's so definitive, there's no room
for gnomes and angels, for nymphs without clits.
Yet, a few men have existed for whom
trees walked in perfect accord with their wits.

This poem in part is written in their praise
and for the bright Light that never decays.

1994

Pastoral

1
Today this field of ripened maize
basks in the bright and holy blaze
of a happy Hasidic sun.
Beneath green stalks though, scared voles run,
frightened by the baleful shadows
of stuka-black Gestapo crows.

2
Borne out of the agonized head
of a scarecrow, racked in my stead,
visions and nightmares encounter
barbed reality, and mount her,
engendering an old despair—
horrible spiders float the air!

3
Where are my ecstatic brethren?
Who's made a hell out of heaven?
Worm that I'd love beneath my foot,
which way's paradise? Mid the soot
at dusk I found but buzzing flies
oozing from almost weeping eyes...

1998

Parallel Universe

The moment when you turned your slouching shoulder
and left the spray of ocean salt behind,
      you entered and you left
      a parallel universe:

      a gull's bill dripping blood
      beneath a sombre cloud,
a dolphin's fin submerged beneath the night,
a tyrant's castle razed by ebbing tide.

      Even if you wanted
      you could not stay or leave.
You yourself have alternate histories
sensual and strange: the man in the moon

walking on your childhood's window pane,
the lilies gasping in the darkness when
      your jack-o'-lantern heart
      first discovers sorrow.

Partisans

They hide in the Naliboki forest,
felling birches, gathering firewood
to heat their hands and kosher porridge.
Stars show the way. They are a good

mile from the sleepy Polish village,
the vale where hate will keep them warm.
Tomorrow they'll rape and kill and pillage,
in twenty years deny all harm.

Tuvia, Aron, Zus, Aseal . . .
names from a Tel Aviv phonebook,
partisans on the movie reel,

heroes who kill Polaks with zeal,
and wash their hands in a cold brook,
as Hollywood tells us what to feel.

Pinocchio

Who is his dim workshop of ageing tears and raspy saws,
in the lull between absinthe and hammers, brothels and nails,
could beget him without sowing a seed in a heartache?

And who will redeem him when fancy has failed lonely eyes,
this pathetic little golem with the soul of a saint
at the threshold of lies and elongated noses?

Though the chalice is empty and bells resound in God's house.
carpenters count their beads in the shade of confessionals,
and, writing in pain, a little puppet hangs on the cross.

1999

Poison

You've reached the nadir and the zenith
        with thoughts that wander meadows
after hours of picking mushrooms.

You cannot count to twenty backwards,
        or remember a tear's
miraculous anatomy,

if it was a drop of dew upon
        a rodent's fingernail,
or sweat upon a tyrant's mug.

You've reached into a cardboard box
        for field corn, crushed it with
your molars, as if a fasting monk,

or a dark and misguided mystic.
        Bells toll behind the bags
of belladonna in the cupboard.

You find yourself alone again
        with grandfather, hands that greet you
the moment the painful ticking stops.

You scan the sea below for land
        to rest your weary talons.
You're a flamingo now, or raven.

Pope Francis

Horny again, Pope Francis
got down on his pink knees,
praying that "Whites finance us."
He invited refugees
whose dark feet, legs and cocks
he washed with nuns from Cisco.
"Not words; such action talks,"
he said, ass full of Crisco.

Poet, Christmas Eve, 1986

He hears incessant jingling in his ear,
but, no, not at the start of some new madness.
Something nears over valleys in the mattress,
and then lands on the rim of his warm beer.

All night it's haunted him like lingering fear,
like flaming tinsel, or Santa Claus's sadness
when he learns that the blonde and blue-eyed waitress
keeps him like a spare, hung and near.

He's taught her English, given her French love,
down on his knees. He's kept her warm and wet,
met the needs that "other" could not meet.

His pockets empty, eyes touched by the dove,
snow melting on the shoulders she won't wed,
the poet weeps and marvels at the feat.

Prayer

Pity us,
too, not much better
than simple apes,

some of us,
aspiring towards
the distant stars

until a Jew
climbed the stained cross,
put us behind

how many thousands
of light years?
Fodder for

bright angels now,
all we have left
is hope and tears.

Promised Land

Rousseau's brave savages
had circled her covered wagon,
leaving vestiges
of life that could have been:

dreams of a promised land,
a son and rag-doll daughter,
a scalped Scottish husband,
and not a drop of water.

Raping her on the prairie
from nightfall to red dawn,
they did not call her "Mary,"
but "whore of the Cheyenne."

They tethered her with rope,
taught her new kinds of pain,
her only living hope:
the fury of white men.

Years later she would watch
the braves flee cannon shot,
the chief squeal like a wretch,
the buffalo meat rot.

Three blows with a hatchet
would prove her only saviour,
a scalped head and a facelift.
And no tears could raise her.

Purple Rain

Mulattoes
drink Muscatel
in the bright glows
of urban hell;

play the fool;
burn the flag;
upon the pole,
watch it wag.

So don't shed tears
Prince had to die.
Some thirty years
had passed him by.
He's with his dears
in a purple sky.

Queue, 1944

Its weathercock covered with fresh snow,
the barn is dreamy on the hill.
Out of the woods, and lying low,
crawl green men, in... in for the kill.

There is no knocking at the door,
only a Mongol's rag-wrapped boot.
He finds her hidden near a store
of oats and rye. She'll be his loot.

The fearsome genes of Ghengis Khan
tell him to grab her by the hair,
red as the sunset on the San,
and ride her flesh like a white mare.

Four inches is enough to slant
the blue eyes of her progeny.
He starts his vodka-reeking pant,
blood on his dirty thigh and knee.

And light, it shines through apertures,
the eyes of needles in the hay.
Whose mother, sister, teacher, nurse
the queue moves toward this Christmas day?

Quick with Flies

It's a tall tale that losers go to heaven,
that victors and blond winners go to hell.
For shines in front of the old Seven-Eleven
judgement was clear: ropes strung, and axes fell.

Who pities hooven swine, the crimson cock,
the crocodile that terrorizes a river?
Was Mister Kurtz correct? Unbolt the lock
and to the parasites give from the giver?

What beasts and ghosts still linger in the mind?
Should we mentor them, and heed their cries?
Can sky-sent miracles change their sad bind?

The stars and moon tell us quite otherwise.
Twenty-seven thousand years behind
in Africa, they're still quick, quick with flies.

Ravens

(Carpathian Mountains)

A flock of carcasses befouls the air
as Bronek counts his losses by a fence.
Two cawing ravens loom above, and their
huge beating wings dispel the awful stench.

The howls he hears usurp his strength of will—
the howls of wolves down through Magora pass.
He stands as stone-faced as the ancient hills,
not knowing whether to move on, or back.

The ravens have descended with the dark
to pounce upon the white entrails of sheep.
And soon with swollen maws they will ascend.

They'll fly to backwoods through a land of stars
still inaccessible to claws and beaks,
a land pure as the dew is innocent.

Refugees
(September 2015)

Ten thousand cuckolds in Iceland
invite ISIS into their beds.
Merkel lifts her heavy hand,
lecturing on conscience, weds
it with betrayal, giving a shove
to Deutschland's honest working poor,
demanding, in the name of love,
that Poland and Hungary take more.
Sobieski turns inside his grave:
"There will be no Europe to save."

Saint Nicholas on the Dole

Before I see his thinning silhouette,
I hear the jingle of his Christmas bell.
Then he coasts round the corner on his Schwinn,
bearing away a starless night's refuse.

Clad now in a coal-black overcoat,
he's left the gem-filled bins to morning dustmen,
to ride off in the sun, heroically,
for a thousand crows still haunt his head.

Sam Gwynn

There once was a good ol' boy and townie,
who, though, ambitious, looked like a half-downie,
who back in college wanted to play ball,
but who, in fact, brought water in the fall
to powerful and fleet black running backs
whom he loved so much, he'd have licked their sacks.
So he took to recycling old stale jokes,
to making fun of kooks and right-wing folks,
to dodging drafts with a fake bum right knee,
to trying not to be a bumpkin flea,
(so he wrote to Dick Wilbur, sought more knowledge,
and found work teaching at a Texas college),
to dining with Dana, hunting with gay Timmy,
assessing in his head: what can they gimme?
However, his old body grew irate
and tumours flowered in his failed prostate.
Now it's a poetry conference he chairs,
attended by old bores and PC squares.

Schultheiss Bierstube

I look down, see there's a new bank
where the *Schultheiss Bierstube* was
the summer of 1934.
It was a place where Germans drank
their *märzen, pilsner, kölsch*. The buzz
of saws in their ears, they would look
out windows on the raised ground floor,
at ducks on the canal, a rook
atop a branch. The barges passed
weighed down with lumber, coal, and steel
on to the Oder railway line.
They drank as long as moments last,
their hopes and dreams expressed in zeal,
hard labour in a mill or mine.
Today, no lager quenches thirst,
no ale cools tongues. The winners of
the war are punished like the cursed,
rooks in the wake of dirty doves.

Seven

Prisoner

The rancid sky
the frail cobweb
the peeling paint
the patient spider
the good book
the hard cock
the naked bulb—

All I know of God
as I enter and re-enter
this prayer.

Down in the Village

Too—the rats snort
their own kind
of nirvana
in the tunnel
to the sad places
behind my eyes,
yon Golgothas
fresh with new crosses
eager to redeem
fallen humanity.

The discarded bags
of chips,
and the busted roaches
of the perpetually
high
know the tedium,

the noble toil
of my closet ascetics
the moment
I set them free.

Mary

She would take it all in,
she would:
the babe and its nostrils,
under the skunk moon
and the pie-eyed stars,
but I hold her in my niche
whispering psalms,
whispering psalms.

Fata Morgana

When I see them
I never doubt it,
though the eyes,
the mortal eyes
sometimes
have visions
mocked by faith.

Sad Old Song

A bird
sable as the heart
on Sunday,

landed on
my right thumb
the moment

I climbed
above despair,

then turned
into a peacock,
rainbow pigeon

when I switched
on the fan.

Rings, Bands, Crosses

They sought brevity,
fresh images.

So they hung a pygmy
from their nostrils,
lips, chins, nipples.

from anything
but their
ears.

Nowhere at Dawn

The star climbed over the edge,
but lacked subtlety,
blazing like an overdose of salt
in the wound of time.

The bones of our ancestors
sank deeper
into our bowels
and no longer
appeared in our dreams.

But we lay stranded,
tethered to a hope,
begging for more.

1999

Sex in the City

She finds herself all by herself in bed,
a web of sunshine on the downy sheet,
a wedding day of bells inside her head,
a layer of cream upon her skin, her feet
still sore from twenty years of love and toil,
yet she thinks that life's been pretty good.
She hears the bacon sizzle, coffee boil
inside the dented pot of spinsterhood.
She has survived the cold and loneliness
of her decisions, and of her mistakes,
proud of her three degrees, no less
than of her freedom. And yet something rakes
her heart inside and leaves her all a mess
and only she herself knows how it aches.

Six Feet beneath the Snow

Deep from head to toe
into the second sleep,
sister to the crow,
she does not hear me weep.

A continent away,
a sky and ocean apart,
I am her last born stray,
I with my leaky heart.

No, we won't ever meet,
resurrected mother,
the shoes now off your feet,
with father, uncle, brother.

Soccer Ball

The soccer ball beneath the lamp—
the noggin of a commissar
the refugees kicked at the camp,
that bounced, but did not roll too far?

What crow picked at its beady eyes
behind a backdrop of deceit,
and bore them over paradise
to open gates, a German street?

And did the trunk, in bloody clothes,
lie like a statue in a pool,
the guillotine hold a red rose
amid the jeers come from the soul?

Sonnet about Liberals

The liberals—
they are the crassest
of criminals.
They see a fascist

when they look at
our Donald Trump.
They don't see fat,
don't see the chump

that's Michael Moore,
don't see the cow
that's Hilary.

Who feeds the poor?
Let them tell how
in the pillory.

Sonnet for All Who Follow Me

Crows and leaves beyond the windowpane,
a cup of steaming coffee on the stool,
my lines reflected in your eyes, which strain
in light as mine once did, the feel of wool
that keeps our stomachs, chests, and shoulders warm
unite us, you now, I who came before.
You wonder how I lived, and ask what harm
beset my age? Floods, earthquakes, famine, war.
Pain transcends the centuries is all
that I can say in speech that has no tenses.
My words part oaks and fly beyond a wall.
They are lamplight reflected in our lenses,
the taste of coffee, cawing in the fall,
the language of the five immortal senses.

Strange Fruit

He's lowered from the tall bright elm,
    neck broken, his gaze hard,
eyes bulging, focused on the realm
    of Christ, his card

recalling rape is a grave sin—
    down South—amid
white-hooded men. His kith and kin
    close each black lid.

They shout "God know" with deer-like eyes
    "he done no wrong."
"Pastor to our church" one cries,
    "Rev. Willie Long."

They loiter in the forest with
    Colt 45,
with crack—as if lost in a myth
    where they still jive.

Sunday Morning

We stand and watch, faith almost wavering,
hunger looking out of childish eyes,
daddy so tall, holding the frightened thing,
head on the block just as the hatchet flies,
falling... fallen by the empty pen,
taking the longest count, as red wings rise,
free at last, and we are saved again.

Susan

Say a prayer for Susan, the sad leper of my tongue.
She taught me the ways of love, how to down hard whisky,
how to watch the rooks above the rowans, ever young
and ready to spread her legs in amorous pity.

Say a prayer for that girl with limbs limp now in the eaves
among the mud of past autumns, among the sins of
whore-masters and cheap fates found in fortune cookies,
among the sweet breaths and buttocks of much-needed
love.

Say a prayer for old whoredom and for the happiness
she gave a few lonely men in the dark for a while.
Say a prayer, say a prayer, for her and good-heartedness.

She flies above the rowans with a flock of rooks now,
flies above my whisky as I long for her living flesh
and have one for her soul as mistaken as her smile.

1998

Tarn Catfish

When viewed from the grey bridge above
they are black submarines that wait
to be refueled. Each collared dove
is their tanked diesel, the sandy shore
of the green isle their pastel plate.

With gaping mouths they drag them down
to the bone yards of pike and bass,
to the cold water, deep and brown,
then they release them at the door
between the clouds that pass and pass.

The Day

The day at last had come.
Twelve guillotines awaited
a queue of pinko scum,
the damned and the ill-fated:

the Marxist prof and fag
with gerbil in his ass,
the feminist old hag
malodorous and crass,

the libtard beta-male
decked out in women's jeans,
the cuck who licked the trail
of other races' genes.

Like mercy fell the sentence,
pure, dutiful and just.
And thus was their repentance,
a heaven red with rust.

The Dickless Sonnet

We heard the formalist recite his verse
in polyester pants. His voice was high,
his tepid lines unmusical and terse.
He wore a polyester clip-on tie
between thin arms with which he would affect
to hold his laboured opus as he bragged
of having studied under Tate and Hecht.
His bald head gleamed, his aging titties sagged.
In silence we all listened. And we looked
at this ambitious little vain castrato
and wondered whether we were being rooked
by one untouched by harp-strings from Erato,
although we knew it is no easy trick
to scribble fourteen lines without a dick.

The Donetsk Morgue
(October 2014)

Some lie alone on carts,
while others who are new,
wait stacked up on the floor.
For you see: there's a queue
inside the Donetsk morgue.

Death masks and private parts
here are processed and tagged,
cadavers on display,
mere torsos, arms and legs,
mouths open, nothing to say.

They can no longer hear
the whistle of big guns,
nor feel guilt in the nude.
Outside, their blood still runs
near where they went for food.

A black crow captures a tear
in the smart phone of its eyes,
and heaven welcomes peace
established by the flies,
and calls for their release.

The End or the Beginning

The sun pours through the window,
honey on her pillow.
She thinks she sees the wind glow,
a blue light on the willow.

Does she hear pure singing,
a songbird on the post?
The end or the beginning,
Mary gives up her ghost.

The Fishmonger's Wife

Eternal in my heart,
she kills the gasping bream.
Never does she depart,
the fish let out a scream.

Poor Mary Magdalene,
mother and old crone,
water trills in the glen
when you cut out the bone.

The Gnosis of Gnomes

A flock of discordant crows quarrelling
at twilight over fallen fruit: their greed's
just part of Jove's plan, as are the fat seeds
stripped of over-ripe flesh, then discarded.

Why the worm writhes in the mud of meadows
and delights in a lack of sun and warmth
only one who lives in clumps of soil
and dung can understand, but's lost his tongue.

Wise men rarely speak, says the man who wrote
all the hieroglyphics and carved the moon's
cratered runes into strophes of darkest light.

Copses give credence, says the smell in the wind.
The quick, as long as they live, know little
of life, till the walls of their minds give in.

1994

The Inferno

I open my window to the flames
and again: the smell of ice and snow
older than the joy of loneliness.

And again: those beautiful black birds,
the rooks, waiting for bits of stale bread
while three storeys high, I cast them spells.

And again: the harsh coughs of gamblers
and visionary loons limping to kiosks,
and the curses of sobering drunks.

And again: the smoke of burning coal
wed to the melancholy rumour
of faintly pealing cathedral bells.

And again: those eternal grey skies,
prostrating, still praying upside down . . .

1998

The Initiate's Song

Caught amid briars and brambles,
clinging to a pillar of salt,
I thought I heard the pale moon sigh
to the glint of a dying star.

But no, it was just the silence
and the brute pounding of my heart:
millenniums of desire,
crocodiles at odds in a swamp.

For wouldn't they, if they but could,
climb out of the senseless cycle,
blue-eyed and upright, like summits
of creation, aspiring?

I thought I saw the stars shed tears,
thought I could pray a way out,
But time gnawed and heaven burned.
boring their way through my crude snout.

1999

The New Bleeding Hearts

They're left behind:
the distant cousin
with feeble mind,
his wife who doesn't
pull up the blind,

both in the dark
with their bad genes,
while we, bold, stark,
spare guillotines,
and, in each park,

help mendicants:
the dazed and drunk
behind on rents,
shines who can dunk
but make no sense.

Like Stroop and Krupp
we tell no lies.
We prop them up
and sterilize;
give soup and cup

and wipe their eyes.

The New Sex

After menopause
the new sex is: back rubs,
an afternoon long nap,
a quarrel about nothing.

The New Sport

Shaming leftists is the new sport:
    the Communist professor,
    the gay nun and confessor,
the tranny on the tennis court,

the emo with so little hope,
    the Feminist who chairs
    other ugly squares,
the media-loving Marxist Pope.

We of the new right beat them down,
    remind them what they are.
    We'll resurrect the Tsar,
and with our wits cause them to frown.

May guilt that stems from new awareness
    whip their unworthy hides.
    Gone are PC free rides.
Our pens will make them bleed with fairness.

The Poet

This winter dawn the grey puddles of ice reflect a mood,
while beneath a shroud the poet's mind sleeps in an igloo.

At the threshold of hell, does he hear the iceman knocking
through the icicles on his earlobes, transcending silence?

Surely he no longer awaits a tryst with dreams, but traipses
with the living dead, searching for the embers of fancy,

or longs for an inn full of warm mead and pale courtesans?
Only Jupiter knows when he's not on a binge with Poe

in the café of codgers and ecstatic charlatans.
For the chimney sweeper would gladly brush him away,

and the rimed satanic bells peal in the frosted garden,
beckoning black water, flocks of Swedenborgian crows,

to cast shadows on the bright hypocrisies of heaven,
though, mute as diamonds—eternity redeems him again.

1999

The Shaman

At the onset of grey time, gathering like storm
over the deformed lull-licking limbs of onyx oaks,
coal-black birds circle the chalcedony of the sky,
looking for mercy where Gabriel would have greeted them.

And, in the conjured waves worshipping the other shore,
the shaman of secrets looks into his burnished stone,
cast down again by the gentle sword of his own death—
for the apocalyptic horses are ever neighing.

Seven years old, I see him weeping in the first light
of every disinherited dawn heaven disowns,
on the banks of the milky river by the grave bridge,
holding his heavy heart in his hand as he jumps in.
And, forever, it seems, he sinks towards oblivion,
like a saviour walking into the depths of a tear.

2000

The Spinning Wheel

Let parasites seize hold of day.
They've always been a part of nature.
Let stink weeds grow high in the garden,
invaders cross the open gate.

But if there's truth, then there's a ray,
a cure upon which we can wager.
Mind and body start to harden,
the spinning wheel restore the state.

The markets come a-tumbling down,
the queen and her three budding shines
go without in the wake of pillage.
And, then, down from the lava hills—

ghosts bear new effigies: a clown
who cuts the gas and power lines,
a knight who pacifies the village,
a saint who closes down the mills.

The Tree-Huggers

There are those who would rather save
a tree than Whites; those who would die
to save a whale, but not a people:
in tall trees, to the buzz of saws,
in little boats, a tidal wave
ahead. Just listen how they cry
in their green church—without a steeple—
saints and martyrs for their cause.
Their gang-banged daughters dead in alleys,
sons hunting in Afghanistan,
still they embrace the boogie nights
and take part in protests and rallies.
They suffer as much as they can,
saviours walking waves, stylites.

The Vale of Spent Tears

It seemed I'd barely slept before I woke.
It was October, or so I gathered
from the embers and the pervasive smoke
of smouldering leaves. A hunchback blathered

philosophically upon a park bench
beckoning rooks and daws with bloodshot eyes.
Impervious to far Gehenna's stench,
I listened, picking out the truths from lies.

My first emphatic love, Melancholy,
like Beatrice with a poppy in her hair,
fed me opium and sweetly lulled me,
and I feigned I saw the Fates in her stare.

Somehow kindred folks smiled and passed us by,
on their way, I supposed, to the same place,
to the grey realm at the edge of the sky,
our reward for having just lost the race.

And yet I wasn't dallying no-where
for nothing. At the corner of two streets
I walked down a dark lager-splattered stair
into a dive full of dwarfs doing feats...

A sad hippie wearing a crown of thorns
hugged me and said that he'd show me the way,
and I swore I could hear trumpets and horns
resounding through all the rainbows of grey...

I asked the Man in charge for a tall malt,
and He served me the da capo sentence:
a blind potato and a fist of salt

mid a choir of angelic stillness...

1996

The Window

As a child I would look out of the window,
     imagining what was on
the other side of January maples:
     a summer lake or pond

with pleasure boats against a sky-blue backdrop,
     over which the sun
shone warmly. Children on the sandy shore
     built castles or would run

as if they were in Eden. No dark clouds
     sailed over the smokestack
of a steelworks, and no soot burned in their eyes
     whenever they looked back.

Tine

There's hard-wrought solitude:
past fifty, out for beer,
alone, not lonely. Ear
attuned to music, food
inside the belly, fine—
knowing dream is better
than a lost love letter,
old teats scrawled with a tine.

Under the Volcano

Fata morgana on the wall
as *los diablos* dance in flame
and more than smoke goes up the chimney.

Yesterday you decided to stop
and now with hills of whisky bottles
behind you, you lie contrite
in acid pools of your own sweat.

The scarred and bleeding liver-priest
inside the temple of your ribcage
no longer purifies your blood.

The tiny silverfish devour
the stems of delicate pink flowers,
and a mouse with the face of Moses
crawls down the paper with the Law.

Widower

I do not ask him why his lips are busted,
his face unshaved and red. I do not question
the stink of last-night's booze, the now dry blood
that stains his flannel shirt. I do not mention
how he looks, or who cannot be trusted.
I know the frog-shit, jaggers, leaves, and mud
on his shoes come from walking all alone
along the river underneath the moon,
wondering why she's dead tonight. His phone
is off the hook and hills of dishes reek,
yet I know the reason's not the reason.
I put the brown bag down and tell him soon
it'll be Thanksgiving, then deer hunting season,
and hug this man too fearful to be weak.

Witness

The wind or consciousness intones:
"Better never to have been born."
You watch along the creek bank stones.
A Norway rat filled up with corn
squeals as a mink drags it away,
the blood left on the loam: a trail,
a trail to heaven, blue today,
but winding first through earth and hell.

What They Found

"The dead came back from Jerusa-
lem, where they found not what they
sought." —Carl Jung, *Seven Sermons to the
Dead*, Sermon I, 1916

Beneath a leaden sky:
street merchants peddling wares,
old harlots exposing breasts,
grimaces and stares,
rats, flies and other pests.

The sun somewhere on high,
its gold not of this earth,
trees, stones and Dead Sea salt,
a fire in an open hearth,
a prayer said to a fault.

So they returned, the glow
within themselves in streams,
the mountain now ascended,
eager to walk our dreams,
knowing all is not ended.

They journey on and grow—
the shimmer of waxed oak,
the bedroom lamp reflected,
the earthquake as you woke
with inner world neglected.

Why Wars Happen, Beings on Earth Die

Above the reeds the red clouds gather.
The boats moored at the river bank
reflect the blood, half full of water.
If only we knew whom to thank.

We look up at the darkening sky,
sun as if sinking, moon aflame,
the figurative language a lie,
and know for sure life is to blame.

Yellow Leaf

When I looked under the yellow leaf
I saw a tear mirroring daybreak,
the chestnut fall of your eyes, the grief
I wear like the mind after the wake.

1999

Your Mother's Eyes, Your Father's Chin

When you kneel down to feed the poor
they've got to have your mother's eyes,
your father's chin. Spurn, curse the Moor.

Muhammad, scornful to the core,
dreams of a Euro Paradise
when you kneel down to feed the poor.

Stupidity is not a cure.
Look at the anger in their eyes,
hate in their mouths. Spurn, curse the Moor.

The haughty Mullah can say more,
on the blond beach, a lord of flies,
when you kneel down to feed the poor.

Lock the front gate and bolt the door;
defend your blood; pray to the skies,
to Mars or Thor. Spurn, curse the Moor.

Love not thy foe, defiant, sure,
you have been fed a pack of lies.
When you kneel down to feed the poor
think of your own. Spurn, curse the Moor.

ABOUT THE AUTHOR

Leo Yankevich was born into a family of Roman Catholic German-Irish-Polish immigrants on October 30, 1961. He grew up and attended high school in Farrell, Pennsylvania, a small steel town in the Rust Belt of Middle America. He then studied History and Polish at Alliance College, Cambridge Springs, Pennsylvania, receiving a BA in 1984. Later that year he travelled to Poland on a fellowship to study at the centuries-old Jagiellonian University in Krakow. A staunch anti-communist, he played an active role in the dissident movement in that country, and was arrested and beaten badly on a few occasions by the Communist security forces. After the fall of the Iron Curtain in 1989, he decided to settle permanently in Poland. Since that time he has lived in Gliwice (Gleiwitz), an industrial city in Upper Silesia.